Yorkshire Mystery Plays

Five medieval plays from the
WAKEFIELD CYCLE

Adapted by
Reg Mitchell

Stratford Playscripts

Yorkshire Mystery Plays was first published in the United Kingdom in 2002
as an original paperback by
Stratford Playscripts
8 Thornton Close
Woodloes Park
Warwick CV43 5XU
United Kingdom
Email: stratfordplayscripts@msn.com

ISBN No: 978 1904232 05 6

Yorkshire Mystery Plays

Five Medieval Plays from the Wakefield Cycle

The Creation

Noah

The Second Shepherds' Play

The Resurrection

The Judgement

Characters

THE BANNS

A Herald or Crier | A Trumpeter

THE CREATION

God | Adam
Eve | Lucifer
Angel Gabriel | Angel 1
Seven non-speaking angels | Angel 2

NOAH

God Noah | Mrs Noah
Three sons | Three wives

THE SECOND SHEPHERDS' PLAY

Coll | Gib
Daw | Mak
Gill | Angel Gabriel
The Virgin Mary

THE RESURRECTION

Pilate | Jesus
Caiaphas | Mary Magdalene
Centurion | Mary Jacobi
Annas | Mary Salome
First Soldier | First Angel
Second Soldier | Second Angel
Third Soldier
Fourth Soldier

THE JUDGEMENT

God | Three Demons
Jesus | Four Evil Souls
Archangel Gabriel | Four Good Souls
Archangel Michael
Lucifer
Peter

YORKSHIRE MYSTERY PLAYS

Yorkshire Mystery Plays were first performed on 4th July 1992,
by **Studio Productions**
in the Crucible Theatre Foyer, Sheffield
then in Orchard Square and in the Abbeydale Industrial Museum,
with the following cast

God	Keith Noble & Ken Scott	Eve	Leslie Cottingham
Adam	Richard Marriott	Lucifer	Ian Gledhill
Noah	Alan Mitchell	Mrs Noah	Sheila Gascoyne
Coll	Chris Rook	Gib	Brian Smalley
Daw	Kevin Daley	Mak	Michael Bullock
Gill	Jenny Derbyshire	Pilate	Charles Ibberson
Caiaphas	Simon Warner	Annas	John Skevington
Mary Magdalene	Jan Wright	Mary Jacobi	Kay Massey
Mary Salome	Sheila Halse	Jesus	Matthew Carter

with

Bob Arkley; Brenda Bell; Kay Brough; Elaine Bullock; Bob Calnan; Mick Connell;
Margaret Davies; Keith Derbyshire; Jill Govier; Chris Heery; John Hughes;
Christine Hunter; Ned Irish; Val Kelsey; Lynda Liddament; Val Mitchell; Jan Millward. Khim
Mortimer; Lynn Nevin; Mark Rose; Gill Stanley; Jack Stevenson; Anne Ward;
Brian Ward; Keith Wathen.

Artistic Director

Reg Mitchell

Pageants directed by

Elaine Bullock
Ian Gledhill
Gill Govier
Mark Rose

Technical Director

Keith Derbyshire

The pageants were sponsored by the local organisations mentioned in the Banns,
which may be amended to suit local circumstances, or omitted altogether

A brief note about the Mystery (or Miracle) Plays

These plays, or pageants, were dramatisations of biblical stories, from The Creation to The Judgement and were popular in the Middle Ages at Whitsuntide - to illustrate the story of the Resurrection. And not only in England, for they enjoyed great popularity on the continent as well. The medieval Church approved the translation of the liturgy into dramatic dialogue in order that the message of man's redemption became clearer to the people. In 1311, the establishment of the Feast of Corpus Christi gave a focus for a form of worship moving away from the liturgy towards performance. So it is hardly surprising that the central focus of the cycles was the Passion of Christ and the resurrection. By the middle of the 14th century, sequences of dramatised biblical stories were being performed all over England. Responsibility for their production was entrusted to the local trade guilds, usually one appropriate to the story. Several sequences of mystery plays have survived. The earliest is probably the Chester cycle, of which twenty-five plays in rhyming verse remain. The York cycle is probably the most complete, with forty-eight plays, again in verse form but of varying expertise. Clearly, several writers were involved in their development; new plays were added from year to year, existing plays revised to keep up-to-date, new guilds came along whilst others declined. The Wakefield cycle, from which these five plays are adapted, has thirty-two plays. Several are very close in content to some of those of the York cycle. Of the Wakefield cycle, nine are in a distinct form of nine-line stanzas by an anonymous writer, referred to as the Wakefield Master. He is generally recognised as the most talented of the writers and most accessible to a modern audience. Noah, and The Second Shepherds' Play in this selection are samples of his comic writing. The increasing secularity of the dramas probably contributed their fall from the Church's acceptance of them. The plays were performed on specially decorated wagons, probably sited in designated open spaces in the town before a festive audience, and to local dignitaries. This gave rise to much competition between the various guilds whose presentations became ever more elaborate and the better actors sought after.

The mystery plays were finally suppressed by the new doctrines of the Reformation and, although they revived for a while during the return to the old ways of Queen Mary's reign, the ecclesiastical authorities of Elizabeth Ist made it deliberately difficult for them to be performed. The corporations of the North of England did not generally welcome their suppression, but were powerless to prevent it. So, at the height of their popularity and dramatic creativity, by the middle of the sixteenth century, they had become defunct. Nevertheless, they formed the bed-rock in the development of the drama, influencing the Tudor and Elizabethan playwrights who followed in their wake.

THE BANNS

A TRUMPETER in medieval attire appears at some vantage point in the area and plays a 'welcome' fanfare, during which a HERALD enters the acting arena on horseback. He unfurls a scroll and reads the Banns.

HERALD   Lordings royal and reverent
                  Lovely ladies that be here evident,
                  Sovereign citizens, hither am I sent
                      With message for you today.
                  I pray you all that be present
                  That you will hear with good intent,
                  And let your ears to be lent
                      Willingly, to what I say.

                  Our worshipful Mayor of this city,
                  For the joy of his fair community   10
                  Solemn pageants ordained hath he
                      At the Festival of Sheffield tide
                  How generous sponsors in his decree
                  Bring forth their plays with ceremony.
                  I shall declare you briefly,
                      If ye will a while abide.

                  The players of Studio Productions
                  Bring forth the heavenly mansion,
                  Hordes of Angels and their creation,
                      According to the finest;   20
                  And when t' angels be made so clear,
                  Then followeth the falling of Lucifer.
                  To bring forth this play with good cheer
                      Musicians be at their best.

                  You backstage men of DIY
                  Look that Paradise be all ready;
                  Prepare also the *Mappa Mundi,*
                      Adam and also Eve.
                  Ye makers of the scenery
                  Look that Noah's Arc be set on high   30
                  That you not hinder the story,
                  And that shall you achieve.

The wardrobe ladies gathered here
Have taken on them with full good cheer
That the Shepherds play shall then appear
    And that with right good will.
Also the Northern General Hospital
Of great trust and reputable,
Offer the Resurrection for your spectacle
    Right fair may be their bill.   40

Dibb Lupton Broomhead, Solicitors three
Of wisdom and prudence, our sponsor be
For T' Day of Judgement to o'ersee.
    No matter what the weather
Tomorrow and next Sunday, without fail
Perform we all, come sun or hail,
In t' Industrial Hamlet at Abbeydale
    These five plays altogether.

Sovereign sirs, to you I say
And to this gathering here today,   50
That performed shall be these goodly plays
    On the fourth after Trinity.
That is, if repeat I may,
Upon the morrow and next Sunday
Who cannot see them all this day.
    In this central vicinity.

Now have I done all that lieth in me
To procure this solemnity,
That these plays continued may be
    And well set forth alway.   60
Jesu Christ sits on high
With his Father in Holy Trinity,
Save all this goodly company
    And keep you all night and day.

The TRUMPETER sounds a fanfare as the HERALD rolls up the scroll and exits. The whole company who are dressed in 'everyday' gear, enter the acting arena in an informal dancing procession, carrying props, skips and sponsorship banners, with the musicians at the fore playing a catchy tune. The musicians take up their places as everyone greets the audience to welcome them to the arena. The cast take their costumes from the skips whilst others set whatever props and settings are needed for the first pageant.

THE CREATION

*As the music ends, there is a fanfare from the trumpeter. The players give way to watch as GOD
appears on high.*

GOD   Ego sum alpha et omega
                       Vita, via, veritas,
                       Primus et nevissimus.
                       It is my will it should be so,
                       It is, it was, it shall be thus

                       (Fanfare.)

                       I am gracious and great God without beginning
                       I am Trinity, which shall have no twinning,
                       The beams of my brightness are blessed in my building,
                       Invisible and visible, all is my welding.

                       A blissful place here will I build   10
                       A heaven without any ending,
                       And angels in nine orders all
                       Upon me be attending.

                       (Fanfare. Nine angels appear on either side of GOD's throne.)

                       Now since I set you by my chair,
                       And brought you here so excellent,
                       See you bring me no despair,
                       Or fall you shall at my intent.

LUCIFER   Nay, Lord, we shall not do that deed,
                       With no wrong doings against thee,
                       Our everlasting life we lead,   20
                       To love thee, Lord, as thy will be.

GOD   Then each be steadfast in your place,
                       And Lucifer, Governor shalt thou be;
                       I grant it now through my good grace,
                       Till I return, be worthy unto me.

                       (GOD exits.)

LUCIFER   Ah! Ah! I am so wond'rous bright,
                    Among you all I shine so clear,
                    For all of heaven, I bear the light,
                    What say you angels that are here?
                    Some comfort I'll take for my fee,   30
                    I'll sit on t' throne and then you'll see,
                    For now I am as great as He.

ANGEL 1   We will not listen to such pride
                    Nor in our hearts have such a thought,

ANGEL 2   None but our Lord shall be our guide,
                    And we keep trust in all he's wrought.

GABRIEL   Our Lord commanded us all here
                    To keep his laws, both more and less,
                    Therefore, I warn thee, Lucifer,
                    Thy pride will turn to great distress.   40

LUCIFER   Distress! I command you all to cease,
                    Look on my beauty now all here,
                    For heaven lights up when I please,
                    God hissen don't shine so clear.

GABRIEL   Alas, that beauty you shall spill
                    The longer pride stays in your thought,
                    For pride will always have its will,
                    And bring your brightness down to nought.

LUCIFER   Behold my friends on every side
                    And unto me now cast your eyes,   50
                    I charge you angels far and wide;
                    Behold and see how I do rise,
                    Above great God I gleam and glide,
                    I am the Governor, none denies;
                    For God himself shines not so wise.
                    I command all angels turn to me,
                    And to your sovereign bend your knee.
                    I am your Lord. Your master. Me!
                    The mightiest of all majesty.

(Consternation among ANGELS. GOD enters.)

GOD   What's all this din that you make here?   60
              Where is your Governor? Hear me call?
              I gave thee charge here Lucifer,
              And now you think you're Lord of all.
              Why sat you here when I did go?
              Have I offended against thee?
              I called you friend. Thou art my foe.
              Why did you do such wrongs to me?
              Above all angels none more-so
              That sat so high in majesty.
              I charge thee fall 'till I say - No,   70
              To t' pits of hell forever be.

(LUCIFER falls from heaven into hell mouth.)

LUCIFER   Alas, that I was ever wrought,
              That I should come into this place;
              I was in joy, now have I nought;
              All forfeit now is all my grace,
              And to this sorrow am I brought;
              The fires of hell now sear my face.

              I vow, therefore, as here I bake,
              To show mankind no joy;
              As soon as ever He can make,   80
              I'll venture to destroy.

              Some of my calling, man shall be,
              And I will make them do amiss;
              I'll work my ways - soon you shall see,
              And keep mankind from heavenly bliss.

(LUCIFER disappears into hell.)

GOD   I regret this case right sorrily,
              Yet still will I have my intent;
              What I first thought so will it be,
              Hark then to my commandment.

Since heaven and earth are made through me,   90
And t' earth is void wi' nought to see,
Then at my bidding, let there be light.
The darkness I name thee - night,

Thus morning and evening, and the first day,
I've made me now as ever I may.
Now will I make a firmament
Amidst the waters to be sent;

The dryness - earth, men shall it call,
Wi' heaven above, beyond, and all:
I will on earth that herbs shall spring;   100
Trees also with fruit forth bring;
Great lights also - I will make two;
The sun and moon - rise up anew;
Stars shall shine through my intent.
Their light on t' earth from me is sent;

Will I in t' water, fish forth bring;
Fowls o'er t' firmament shall wing,
And beasts I bid will multiply,
In t' earth - in t' water - bye and bye.
So come, let praise attend,   110
How all is made from nought
Beginning - midst - and end,
I, with a word have wrought.

On t' seventh morn I mean to rest,
In t' knowledge that I've done my best,
But this the sixth, a beast of skill I'll make,
In t' shape of me and my likeness
And which shall worship to me take.
Of t' dullest dust on earth that is here,
I shall make - MAN.   120
Rise up then dust, in blood and bone,
In t' shape of man, I command thee.

(ADAM burst through the gravel.)

12

A female now - to play her part;
From his left rib, now shall I make;
(EVE bursts through the gravel.)

Share each the comforts of your heart,
And be ye fruitful, for my sake.
Take now here the ghost of life,
And receive both your souls of me.
Take this female to thy wife:
Adam, and Eve, your names shall be.   130

Adam and Eve, this is the place
That I have made thee through my grace
To make your living in.
Herbs, spice, fruit on t' tree,
Beasts, fowls, all that you see,
You master all herein.
This place is Paradise;
Here shall your joys begin.

ADAM   Oh, Lord, to whom all things are known,
We thank you for this joyful home   140
That you have brought us to:
Full of solace, calm and mirth,
Everything we need on earth -
And spices even too.
Look Eve, and see this sight,
What need we less or more,
But live and praise Him right
And cherish all this store.

EVE   It is a joyful sight;
We here in peace shall dwell.   150
We love thee God of might,
And mean to do right well.

GOD   Love my name with good intent
And hark to my commandment;
My bidding both obey.
In Paradise, all fruit you see

Is thine to taste right happily,
Bar one; the tree of good and ill.
If thou should eat of this,
Thou goes against my will   160
And be banished from my bliss.

ADAM   Alas, Lord, that we should do such ill.
        Thy bidding we shall both fulfil.
        That tree we will not touch or taste
        Lest all our joys be brought to waste.

EVE   Thy bidding we shall do,
        And worthy shall we be.
        That fruit forbid by you
        Will hang still on that tree.

GOD   Now all is made that I began,   170
        And t' sixth day done, so will I rest;
        My work is ended now, at man,
        And I've done well - but this is t' best.
        Adam and Eve thy wife
        'Tis time I bid good cheer;
        With joy now lead your life,
        And blessing have you here.

        (GOD exits. Enter LUCIFER. ADAM and EVE sleep.)

LUCIFER For woe, my wits are in a whirl
        That grieves me greatly in my mind.
        For He from heaven did me hurl,   180
        And now he riles me wi' mankind.
        In Eden now they both abide;
        With wily ways I will them stain;
        In a worm's likeness will I glide,
        To Adam's mate I'll ply some pain.

        (LUCIFER goes but re-enters as a dragon.)

        See how right wormily I wend.
        Eve! Eve!

EVE   Who's there?

LUCIFER   I, a friend. *(The SERPENT dances.)*

     Of all the fruit that you see hang
     In Paradise, why eat ye nought?

EVE   We may eat every one,   190
     But one tree we are taught.

LUCIFER   And why that tree? I ask of you,
     Any more than all t' others close by?

EVE   For our Lord, God forbids us to.
     The fruit, he said, that Adam nor I
     Should eat it not;
     And if we do, we both should die,
     He said, and lose all we have got.

LUCIFER   Yah Eve! Listen to me.
     I know his skill - I know his way.   200
     That tree that He calls good and ill;
     Eat it safely you may.
     The fruit of knowledge lies therein;
     He would not wish it top be known,
     For who would eat and knowledge win;
     Might have more knowledge than His own.

EVE   Why, what thing art thou,
     That tells this tale to me?

LUCIFER   A worm, that knows well how
     That you may worshipped be.   210

EVE   What worship do I want to see?
     To eat that fruit I want it not
     We're here with all our mastery
     Of everything that earth has got.

LUCIFER   Woman, do way.
To greater heights you may be brought,
If you will do what I will

EVE   To do that is not right;
To treat our God that way.

LUCIFER   Nay! Nay! Now don't tek fright;   220
Eat it safely you may.
No pain or peril therein lies,
But honour and some great winning;
For just like God, you shall be wise,
And t' same as him in everything.
Aye, Gods shall you be.

EVE   Is this the truth you say?

LUCIFER   Why, Eve, you can trust me,
I'd never, not in no way
Tell owt but truth to thee.   230

EVE   Then I shall tek thee at thy word,
And tek this fruit here for some food.

(EVE plucks an apple from the tree.)

LUCIFER   Bite on boldly, don't be scared,(She bites.)
And give Adam some, to help his mood,
And bring him blissss.

(She wakes ADAM as LUCIFER glides away giggling.)

EVE   Adam, have here some fruit right good.

ADAM   Alas, woman, why took thou this?
Our Lord commanded us
To leave this tree of his.
Alas, thou does amiss.   240

EVE   Nay, Adam, do not fear,

And I shall tell you t' reason why -
A worm has brought some merry cheer;
We shall be gods you and I;
We shall be as wise
As God that is so great,
And all through this prize;
Come on Adam - eat.

ADAM A worm, it was said what to do?
Eh, I'm not sure I dare.   **250**

EVE Bite on boldly, for it's true.
We shall be gods without a care.

ADAM To win that name, I shall it taste.

(He bites - the SERPENT is convulsed with laughter.)

Alas, what have I done for shame?
I knew I shou'n't have trusted thee.
Eve, thou art to blame;
To this tha' tempted me.

My body does me shame,
For I am naked and all bare.

EVE Alas, Adam, and so am I.   **260**

ADAM In sorrows soon might we both share;
For we have grieved God Almighty
That made man;
Broken his bidding bitterly -
Alas, that ever it began.
This work, Eve, falls thy lot, -
Thou 'st made this a bad bargain.

EVE Nay, Adam; blame me not.

ADAM Goo way, love Eve; who then?

EVE	That worm's to blame; he tricked me here,	270
	Wi' tales untrue I was betrayed.	
ADAM	Alas, that I listened and let thee draw near;	
	I regret to my sorrow this plot that's been played.	
	My body shakes and grieves.	
	How can it best be hid?	
EVE	Let us take these fig leaves,	
	Some shame at least to rid.	
ADAM	Right as you say, so shall it be,	
	For we are naked and all bare.	
	I wish that I could hide me	280
	From my Lord's sight - if I knew where -	
	Where I don't care.	

(GOD appears with GABRIEL by his side.)

GOD	Adam! Adam!	
ADAM	Lord, I hear thee, but see thee not.	
GOD	Say, who does it belong	
	This work? Why hast thou wrought?	
ADAM	Lord, Eve made me do wrong,	
	And to this brink has brought.	
GOD	Say, Eve, why did you make your mate	
	Eat fruit I told thee should hang still,	
	And commanded none of it to take?	290
EVE	A worm, Lord, enticed me until -	
	Alas for shame	
	That ever I did a deed so ill.	
GOD	Ah, wicked worm, thou'll pay right dear	
	For causing this 'ere mad affray.	

My vengeance have you here.
With all the might I may.

(GOD zaps the SERPENT - it collapses.)

On your belly shall you slide,
And be ye known right hatefully
To all mankind on every side.   300

(SERPENT crawls off on all fours.)

And t' earth it shall thy sustenance be
To eat and drink.
Adam and Eve, also ye
In earth then shall you sweat and shrink
And forage for your food.

ADAM   Alas, then might we sink.
            All t' world was ours to suit our mood,
            Now grievously we slink.

GOD   Come, Cherubim, my angel bright,
            To t' middle earth go drive these two.   310

(GABRIEL descends.)

GABRIEL   All ready, Lord, as it is right,
            Since thy will is that it be so
            And thy liking.
            Adam and Eve, you two must go,
            Here may you make no dwelling.
            Go ye forth fast, to fare;
            Of sorrow you may sing.

ADAM   Alas, for sorrow and care,
            Our hands we wring;   320
            For put we were in great plenty
            At prime o' t' day.
            By time of noon all lost had we;
            So we'll away.

19

(ADAM and EVE exit.)

(GABRIEL gestures to the musicians who immediately play as GABRIEL exits into Heaven. It is a song of sorrow and regret. Probably 'Lay Me Low' (John Tams) Some sing the song as the cast change out of costumes and exit with skip whilst others clear props and setting.)

During the song, the CAST OF NOAH enter the acting arena with sponsor banner, props and skip and put on costumes as others arrange the setting and props. They retire as NOAH comes forward to talk to the audience.

NOAH

NOAH   Tha' knows that our gracious Lord, in his likeness, made man,
          That rank to be restored, even as it began,
          Of the trinity by accord; Adam, and Eve that woman
          To multiply without discord, put He in Paradise, an'
              To each one both
          In commandment said
          On the tree of life no hand be laid;
          But the false fiend did persuade
              And though at first right loathe,

          Enticed man to gluttony, stirred him to sin of pride,   10
          But in Paradise securely, might no sin abide,
          Sith now, before His sight, every living man
          Most part of day and night, sin in word and deed
              Full bold;
          Some in pride, ire and envy,
          Some in covetousness and gluttony,
          Some in sloth and lechery,
              And in other wise many fold.

          Therefore, I dread lest God on us will be revenged
          For sin is now aloud without any pretend.   20
          Six hundred years and odd have I, without doubten
          On earth, as any sod, lived with great burden
              Always;
          And now I wax old
          Sick, sorry and cold,
          As muck upon mould
              I wither away;

          An' yet I mun cry for mercy and call,
          Noah thy servant am I, Lord, ower all !
          Lest me and my wife and fry shall fall;   30
          Save us from villainy and bring to thy hall
              In heaven;
          And keep me from sin,
          This world within;
          Comely king of us all,
              I pray thee, hear my call.

(GOD appears above.)

GOD   Sin' I have made all things that do live and stand,
Every man, at my beck should obey my command.
Man showed I love when I made him as me
But now in disgrace full low lieth he.   40
   On this fall,
Vengeance will I take
On earth for sin's sake;
My wrath shall I wake
   On creatures all.

I repent that day that ever I made man;
He will not me obey, though I am his sovereign;
Therefore will I destroy all that do stand.

(Enter Mrs NOAH.)

All shall perish, by my ordering,
   That ill has done.   50
On earth I see right nought
But sin that is unsought;
Of those that good has wrought
   Find I hardly none.

Therefore shall I undo all earthly thing
Wi' floods that shall flow, and rains shall I bring -
For sin on earth is all abroad.
Thus I with vengeance, draw my sword,
   And make an end
To all that bears life.   60

(Enter NOAH.)

Save Noah and his wife;
For they would never strive
   With malice to offend.

(GOD descends.)

To Noah shall I go
And warn him of this woe.

Noah, my friend, for thy sake I shall thee shield;
A ship I bid thee make, of nail and board, right well.
Thou allus was a good worker, and to me true as steel;
At my word obedient, thus my friendship shall thou feel
    As thy reward.   70
In length thy ship should be
Three hundred cubits; put trust in me;
In height, even thirty,
    And of fifty broad.

NOAH   Who art thou to tell what shall be? I pray thee ?
Thou art full marvellous thee,
Tell me I pray, Thy name so graciously.

GOD   My name is full glorious and of dignity
    To know;
(Reveals himself to NOAH.)
I am God most mighty;   80
I made thee and all men to be.
Thy obedience to me
    Thou shoulds't show.
(NOAH falls to his knees.)

NOAH   I thank you Lord, so dear, you will us save
And here on t' ground appear, to me a simple knave;
Bless us Lord here, for charity I crave;
The better we may steer, that ship upon the wave
    For certain.

GOD   Noah, to thee and thy crew,
My blessings are due;   90
You shall multiply anew
    And fill the earth again,
When all those floods are past and fully gone away.

(GOD exits.)

NOAH
I shall homeward in haste as fast as I may,
And my wife greet, with tales of the day;
I hope she spins sweet; she can cause much affray
    And chastise me;
For she bites sharply;
If anything be awry,   100
She can be right angry,
    So ! soon shall I see.

Now then my dear - how do?

MRS NOAH No better for seeing thee; that's true.
Thou brings home no fare, I rue,
That we all be starved, by you;
    But for me.
While I sweat and shrink,
Thou does just as tha' thinks.
Yet of meat and of drink   110
    In much need are we.

(Addresses women in audience.)

We women must harry all poor husbands;
An' I have one, by our Mary, that demands -
If he's troubled I must tarry, whilever it stands,
With pretence of worry and wringing me hands
    For fear;
But still otherwise
With game and with guile,
I shall smite and smile,   120
    And pay him back dear.

NOAH   Hold thy tongue, clatter-trap, or shall I it still.

MRS NOAH Why if tha' gives me a slap; repay it I will.

NOAH   My patience will snap; have at thee, Gill.

(Going to slap her.)

MRS NOAH   Stick that in thee cap! And that if tha will!

   (Slaps him twice.)

NOAH   Ah, wilt thou so do!

   There's one *(Slaps her.)* and again. *(And again.)*

MRS NOAH   Thou'lt have three for thy two; I swear by God's
   pain.

NOAH   An' I shall quieten thee though, i'faith that's plain.

MRS NOAH   Out upon thee; Ho !   130

NOAH   Hold! I will keep charity for I have much to do.

MRS NOAH   There's none here that keep thee. Good riddance to you.
   Full well may we miss thee. Sod off - cheerio.
   You do as you like; to spin will I go.

NOAH   Well farewell, missus !
   To work must I flee for time draws an end;
   My gear must I fetch, and my bones must I bend -
   I trust that the Trinity some succour will send.
      I wiss us.

   What know I of arkwrightery ?   140

   *(He kneels to pray. As he prays, the musicians play a suitable tune during which,
   the ark appears drawn on by the THREE SONS and THEIR WIVES.)*

NOAH   He said all shall be slain, but only we,
   Our bairns that obey us, an' their wives three;
   A ship he bade me create to save us to see;
      Lord ! We thank thee.

ALL   Amen

25

NOAH   Be not afeared. Have done! Pack up our gear,
     That we be safe without more fear.

1st SON   It'll be done, I swear.

2nd SON   Brother, help to carry.

NOAH   Dear wife; come in t' ship at my bidding.

MRS NOAH   Noah, my strife, go from t' door to the middin.

1st WIFE   Good mother, come in straight way, for all's overcast;   150
     Both the sun and the moon

2nd WIFE   and mighty winds blast
       Full sore.
     They make such a din,
     Therefore, mother, come in.

MRS NOAH   No! I'm sat here to spin.
       Give o'er.

3rd WIFE   If you like, you may spin, mother, in t' ship,

NOAH   Come in, afore from t' hill we away slip

MRS NOAH   Aye. The waters now I can see. Oh, I sit not dry.
     Into t' ship will I flee as fleet as I can fly;   160
       Or else I drowned be.

(She addresses women in audience.)

     Lord, I'd be better pleased for a mercy small,
     If I could but dress in a widow's shawl;
     So would most, more or less that I see in this hall

NOAH   *(He bellows at her.)* Gill! Come in! For charity !

MRS NOAH   Among lasses here wed
     For the lives that they've led
     Wish their husbands were dead;

> For it has to be said,
> > I wish that mine were.   170

NOAH *(Addressing the men.)*
> You men that have wives, while they are young
> If you respect your own lives, chastise their tongue.
> I think my heart sighs, and me liver and lung,
> to hear t' sorry cries from t' married men among.
> But I
> > As have I bliss,
> > Shall chastise this

MRS NOAH Yet may ye miss
> > Y' gert Nelly !

NOAH I shall make thee still as stone, beginner of blunder!   180
> I shall beat thee black and blue, and break all asunder.

> *(They fight.)*

MRS NOAH Out alas, I am overthrown! Out upon thee man's wonder!

NOAH See how she can groan, and I lie under;
> > But wife,
> > Let's have no more ado,
> > For my back's near in two.

MRS NOAH And I am beaten so blue
> > And wish for no more strife.

> *(THE SONS enter the ark.)*

1st SON Ay! Why fare you thus? Dad and Ma both!

2nd SON Your spite would scarce free us from such sin as wroth.   190

3rd SON These scenes are so hideous, I swear on my oath.

NOAH We will do as ye bid us, and that with no sloth.
> > Dear bairns!

Now to the helm will I walk
And tend to the ark.

MRS NOAH   I see in the sky dark
      Methinks, the Great Bear.

(Storm music.)

(The arc is buffeted in the storm and trucked around the acting arena if possible during the storm and music. The next few cues are spoken over the storm effect.)

NOAH   This is a great flood; wife, tek heed.

MRS NOAH   So I thought as I stood. We are in great dread.
      These waves are so high;

NOAH   Help, God, in our need;   200
      As thou art a good helmsman, t' best as I reed
        Of all;
      Save us in this race,
      As thou did promise.

MRS NOAH   This is a perilous case.
      Hear, God, when we call

(The storm begins to abate. Music continues as NOAH FAMILY mime the easing of the buffeting.)

NOAH   Wife, tend the tiller, and I shall assay
      The depth of the sea that we bear if I may.

MRS NOAH   That shall I do full wisely. Now, go thy way,
      For upon this flood have we floated many a day,   210
        With pain.

NOAH   Now the water will I sound
      Ah ! It's very far to the ground;
      This labour I expound
        Had I t' time.

Above all hills indeed, the water is risen o'er
Fifteen cubits . But it shall no more
I think, for this cannot be, I know, for
After forty days of rain it'll start to lower -
    Full truly.   220
The water's depth
Again will I test;
Aye ! Now can we rest
    For it's waning most surely.

(Musicians sing while NOAH takes sounding and family go about their business.)

NOAH   Now forty days of rain are ceased and t' cataracts up-knit,
                But sithee t' sun is shining through t' clouds, isn't it?

MRS NOAH Aye ! T' tops of hills I can see, that's a gradely sight.
                My eyes must shielded be, the day is so bright.

NOAH   Wife, prithee !
                What bird might be best, with speed of its wing,   230
                From t' east or from t' west some token to bring
                Without tarrying ?
                    Counsel me !

(Musicians play or sing as Mrs NOAH dips inside the ark and reappears with cupped hands. She passes the mimed dove to NOAH who releases it. A white umbrella is flapped like wing beats.)

NOAH   This is the first day of the tenth moon.

MRS NOAH The dove, durst I say will come back very soon.

(Umbrella beats return of bird.)

Look here, I say, look! She is coming ere noon -
And bringing in her bill some tidings too.
    D' y' see ?
It's taken from an olive tree -
A branch, it seems to me.   240

NOAH	Right true, dear wife; It be !
	Saved are we !

1st SON	The floods, father, are gone, behold.

2nd SON	There is left hardly none, and that ye be bold.

3rd SON	As still as a stone, our ship has firm hold.

NOAH On land here has run; God's grace is untold;
    My children dear,
Shem, Japhet and Ham,
With glee and with game,
Go we in God's name,   250
    No longer abide here.

Good living let us now begin
So that we grieve our God no more.

He set this rainbow clearly then
As knowledge to all Christian men,
With waters he'd ne'er waste again.
Thus has God most of might
    Set up his sign full clear,
Up in the air on height;
His rainbow it is right,   260
That men may see this sight,
    In t' season of the year.

(The musicians play or sing a joyful song which members of the cast can join in as the cast change costume and the skip, props and the arc are removed from the arena.)

END

THE SECOND SHEPHERD'S PLAY

During the song, the cast come into the arena with banner, skip and props. The cast put on costumes as necessary, whilst others set props and setting. COL comes forward as others retire; he is trying to keep warm and singing.

COLL   Lord! But this weather's so cold! And I'm so badly wrapped.
                I'm stiff wi' cold so long have I napped;
                My legs'll hardly hold; my fingers are chapped!
                I'm getting too old and I am all lapped
                    Wi' sorrow!
                In storms and tempest,
                Now in the east, now in the west,
                It's hard luck on 'im as can't rest
                    Today nor tomorrow!

                But we poor shepherds that walk on the moor   10
                We're no better than t' farm hands turned out o't' door.
                Small wonder, as it stands, that we be poor,
                Best part of our lands lies as fallow as the floor,
                    As ye ken.
                We are so pushed,
                O'ertaxed and crushed,
                We're all but bust
                  By these gentry men.

                It does me good, as I walk thus by mine own,
                Of this world to talk in manner of moan.
                                                          20

                (Enter GIB frozen almost to death.)

GIB   Lord! This weather's so spiteful, and the winds like ice,
                And the frost's so frightful it water's me eyes -
                    No joke!
                Now in dry, now in wet,
                Now in snow, now in sleet,
                When my shoes freeze to my feet
                  It's not easy, folk.

COLL   Oi! look over here; you there! are ye deaf!

GIB   Yea, the devil in thy maw - in tarrying

Hast ye seen Daw   30

COLL   Yea, on the lea land
        I heard him blow. He comes here at hand,
            Not far.   Stand still!

GIB   Why?

COLL   For he comes, nearby.

GIB   He'll fool us with a lie
            I expect - or he'll try!

(Enter DAW - a young shepherd.)

DAW   Ah, sir! God you save, and master mine!
        A drink I really crave and on summat to dine.

COLL   By heck, you lazy knave, your belly'll regret it   40

GIB   How the lad loves to rave and any road,
            We've ate it.

COLL   Bad luck on your pate!
        Though the lad came late,
        Yet is he in state
            To dine - if he had it.

DAW   Such servants as I, that sweat and swear
        Eat our bread full dry, and that's unfair.

GIB   Peace, lad, I say. No more jangling,
        Or tha'll regret it, by the heaven's king!   50
            Say I.

COLL   Aye! By the rood, these nights are long!
        Yet I would, ere we go, someone gave us a song.

GIB   Aye, one we all know, we can all join along

COLL   T' tenor part, I

GIB   And me t' treble right high.

DAW   Then t' other I'll try.
               Let see how we fare.

(They sing a brief canon. Mak enters singing with them)

COLL   Who's that who pipes so poor

(MAK appears and puts on posh voice.)

MAK   None but a lord that walks on the moor   60

(MAK sniggers and hides.)

GIB   Mak, where 'as tha gone ?
              Tell us tidings.

DAW   As he comes, then each one, look after your things.

MAK   What ? I be a yeoman I tell you of the King;
              A messenger royal. Great news I bring.

COLL   Nay!

GIB   Give over!

DAW   Come on Mak!

MAK   I shall make complaint - so beware forsooth,
              If I hear another word.

COLL   Mak, take out that Southern tooth
              And tuck it in a turd.   70

MAK   Nay, lads, it's only me tha knows.
              How goes you; how's the herd ? *(He joins them.)*

GIB   Now listen, you fraud;
     Thus late as tha goes,
     What might we suppose ?
     For we all on us knows
     There's sheep stealing abroad.

MAK   But I am true as steel,
     Tha knows that I'm straight -
     It's a sickness I feel
     And it roars in me great.   80
     My belly won't heal -
     It's in a right state.

COLL   If you're after a meal lad,
     You've got here too late -

GIB   That's for sure.

MAK   As I stand here, stone still
     All ravaged and ill,
     I've ate nowt but a quail;
     This month or more.

GIB   Mak, how's thee wife ?   90
     Come on; tell us all here,
     How does she do ?

MAK   Lies lathering by t' fire -
     Languishing low -
     And t' house full of our brood
     And she drinks well too.
     I've tried as hard as I may,
     But there's nowt I can do -
       Aye it's true.
     She eats as fast as she can   100
     And each year that comes to man
     She brings forth an infant;
       And some years - two.

(The others grow bored and doze.)

If I were wealthy wi' treasures unknown
She'd still eat me out of house and of home.
And she's such a foul mouth if you come near;
There's no man from the South to the North
    Knows suffering like I.
If I had more to proffer
I'd give all in my coffer
At tomorrow's mass to offer
    A penny, should she die.   110

COLL   Eh! I'm that weary wi' waking as none in this shire;
             I'm not paid enough to be stuck in this mire.

GIB   I'm cold and I'm shiv'ring - I could do wi' a fire.

DAW   I'm worn out wi' walking - and about to expire.

COLL   Hey! You keep awake.

             (He lies down.)

GIB   Nay! Down must I lie;
             Sleep catches me eye.

             (He lies down.)

DAW   If it's alright for you   120
             I'll give it a try.

             (He lies down but remembers MAK.)

             Hey! Mak, come here, between us shall tha' lie.

MAK   If I draw up right near, on your plans I might spy;
             So tek heed.

             (He lies down - and pops up again.)

             From my top to my toe,

Manus tuas commendo,
Pontio Pilato,
Christ's cross me speed.

(They all cross themselves and sleep. MAK begins to draw a spell on the sleepers, drawing a circle round them.)

About you a circle as round as a moon,
'Til I've done what I will, until it be noon.   130
Now lie here stone still until it is done,
And stay here at rest til the rays of the sun
    Are on height.
O'er your heads my hands I wave;
Out go your eyes, your sight to save;
For I must away, your blessings I crave.

(The SHEPHERDS grunt in their sleep.)

    This working is right.

See how they sleep hard, that may you all hear -

(The SHEPHERDS snore.)

I was never a shepherd, but now will I learn.
The flock might be scared, so I'll nimbly nip near -   140

(MAK approaches a lamb.)

Baa! Come hitherward - that's changed all me cheer
    From sorrow.
A Fat sheep I dare say,
A good fleece, gone astray,
Pay back when I may -
    But this I will borrow.

(MAK goes to his cottage.)

Eyup Gill, art thou in? Gi' us some light

36

GILL   Who meks such a din this time o' the night?

MAK   Wife, oppen up quick. Can't you see what I bring?

GILL   I shall oppen the sneck.   150

(MAK 'enters'.)

GILL (cont) Ah, come in my sweet thing.

MAK   Thus it fell to my lot Gill; I had such grace.

GILL   Aye, gracious or not - we'll be hanged for this case.

MAK   Oh, I wish it were slain; I'm right ready to eat:
                  This twelve month, oh the pain for a slice of sheep meat.

GILL   And suppose it's not slain and they hear the sheep bleat?

MAK   Then I might be ta'en. Tha's gi'n me cold feet.
                  Go bar the back door.

(She does.)

GILL   A good jest have I spied, since thou can find none:
                  Here shall I him hide, until they are gone   160
                  In this cradle - abide - then let me alone.
                  And I shall sit down beside as in childbirth and groan.

MAK   Well said!
                  And I shall say that you've had
                  Of a child this night - a young lad.

GILL   (To audience.) This is a good guise - our troubles are past.
                  Still, a woman's advice helps at the last.

MAK   The last words they said when I turned me back:
                  They would see that they had all their sheep in the pack.
                  They'll not be well pleased if they any sheep lack.   170

GILL   Hark, when they call; for they'll come all at once.

Then mek ready all and sing on thy own;
Sing 'Lullay, Lullay' and I shall just groan
And cry out on t'wall wi' merciless moan
    Right sore.

COLL   Alas, come wake from your sleep -
We're fools to a man -
We've lost us a sheep.

GIB   By heck! Not that lamb ?

DAW   Trust me if you will -   180
I bet all I've got -
It's Mak or their Gill
That's behind this 'ere plot.

COLL   Then away we must tread and run on our feet.
I shall never eat bread till I ditch this deceit.

GIB   Nor drink in my head till with him I meet.

DAW   I'll rest in no bed, until I him greet.

*(THE SHEPHERDS approach MAK's house; MAK sees them coming and starts
singing the lullaby but GILL doesn't hear the signal; MAK sings louder still until
GILL responds with moans and groans.)*

MAK   Why sirs, what ails ye, owt but good ?

COLL   Aye! Our sheep that we keep
Are stole as they goes.   190
Right angry we be.

GIB   Mak, some men suppose it could be thee.

DAW   Either thee or thy spouse; so say we.

MAK   How can you suppose that of Gill or of me ?
Come, rip oppen our house and then you may see
Who had her.

If we've any sheep got
Either female or tup -
and Gill my wife rose not
Here since she laid her -   200
As I am true and loyal, to God here I pray
That this be the first meal that I eat this day.

(The sheep bleats.)

GILL   Ooh! Me middle.
I pray to God so mild
If ever I thee beguiled,
That I eat this child
That lies in this cradle.

(The sheep bleats - GILL moans.)

MAK   Peace woman, for God's pain and cry not so.
Tha' addles thi brain and makes me full woe.   210

GIB   I'm sure our sheep be slain; I think we should go.

DAW   All our work is in vain; as well may we know.
There's just tatters.
I can find no flesh,
Hard or nesh,
Salt or fresh -
Only two empty platters.

(Points to cradle.)

Living beast, besides this, tame or wild,
None, as I have bliss, though it smells a bit mild.

GILL   No. So God gi' me bliss and bring joy to me child.   220

COLL   Our working's amiss. I think we're beguiled.

GIB   Sir, we've done.
But Sir - Our Lady save him -

Is your child girl or knave ?

MAK   Any Lord might him have,
           This child, as a son.

GIB   Mak, friends will we be
           For we are all one.

(GIB offers his hand - MAK rejects it.)

MAK   We ? Nay, I hold back, me -
           For amends get I none.   230
           Farewell all three.

(The shamefaced SHEPHERDS leave.)

(Aside.) I'm glad that they've gone.

DAW   Fair words may there be, but love is there none
             This year.

COLL   Did you give the bairn anything ?

GIB   Why no; not one farthing.

DAW   Fast again will I fling:
             I'll see you both there.

(DAW runs back to the cottage.)

Mak, take no more grief if I come to they bairn.

MAK   Nay, tha' called me a thief, and now it's my turn.

DAW   Thy child must not grieve, that little day star.   240
           Mak, with your leave, let me give your bairn
             But sixpence.

MAK   Nay, have done, he sleeps.

DAW   I think he peeps.

MAK   When he wakens he weeps.
             I told you - go hence.

DAW   Let me give him a kiss,
             I'll not wake him, don't doubt.

             (He goes to the crib.)   What the devil is this ?
             He has a long snout.   250

COLL   He's marked all amiss.
             We should not pry about.

             (He heads Daw away.)

GIB   Ill-spun weft like this allus comes foul out. *(He takes a look.)*

             Aye so.

             (GIB gives MAK a 'tough luck' smile - joins other two.)

             He's a bit like a sheep.

DAW   Oh, let's have a peep.

             (CLOO and GIB stop DAW going.)

COLL   Nature runs deep -
             It's as well we don't know.

             (The baby bleats. SHEPHERDS look at crib - then at one another - then at the crib.)

GIB   *(Lamb bleats again.)* So that's your game -
             Your craft is cast.   260
             There's the shame.

             (GILL and MAK have taken the lamb from the crib and are backing away - the SHEPHERDS slowly pursue them.)

COLL   Aye, a pretty past.
              Let's dunk this dame and bind her fast
              For now the blame comes home at last.
              Hold thy row.

DAW   Does t' see how they swaddle
              His four feet in the middle ?
              I never saw in a cradle
              A horned lad 'til now.

MAK   Peace, bid I. What! Let be your uproar.   270
              I'm the one that him got and yon woman him bore.

GIB   Let be all that rot.
              I've told thee before.
                I saw.

GILL   A pretty child as he
              Ne'er sat on mother's knee;
              A simple-dolly-dee,
              That makes his daddy laugh.

DAW   I know him by the ear mark:
              That is a sure token.   280

(The SHEPHERDS close in.)

MAK   I tell you, sirs - hark - his nose was broken
              Then told me a clerk, some witchcraft was spoken.

COLL   This is a false work; revenge is awoken.
                Get weapon.

(SHEPHERDS raise crooks and close in on MAK.)

GILL   He was taken by an elf;
              I saw it meself -
              When the clock struck twelve
                Was he mis-shapen.

(DIB grabs the lamb.)

GIB   You're one and the same, and should lie in one bed.

COLL   If they deny all the blame, let's do 'em both dead.   290

MAK   If I trespass again, then chop off me head.

            (To audience.) With you judgement remain.

            (DAW leads off GILL and lamb while the others hold MAK firm and parade him round.)

COLL   Since Mak for his sin has caused such affray;
            Then it's best we begin and reward this display -

GIB   He thought he might win, and dine dainty all day,
            So we'll feed him within; and without I dare say;
                On his chops.

            (Daw returns with 'slosh'.)

COLL   Some porridge might do ?

GIB   Or a plate of cold stew ?

DAW   He's in custardy, true.   300
            We'll serve him wi' slops.

            (MAK is sloshed, wrapped in slosh cloths and bundled out by DIB and DAW to the accompaniment of suitable music.)

COLL   Lord, I am right sore, at point for to burst.
            I can't manage one step more, I must lie down here first.

GIB   *(Returning.)* I'm dead beat upon this floor; for sleep I have great thirst
            I would gladly roll me o'er and in t' thistles I'll be nursed.

DAW   Now I pray you -
            Try this for thy bed. *(Indicates a suitable space.)*

COLL   These thieves still run in me head.

DAW   Just lay down and be said;
     Come on! Do as I say you.

(They lay down to sleep. The musicians play heavenly music, 'wonder, curious, wi'
small notes among', during which the ANGEL GABRIEL descends and speaks
over.)

GABRIEL Hark, shepherds, here,   310
     You needest not fear
     Of this star that you see;
     For this same morn
     God's son is born
     In Bethlehem of a maiden free.
     Go haste ye there with hearts right high;
     It is His will you shall him see
     Between two beasts, he waits for thee.

(GABRIEL ascends.)

(The VIRGIN MARY and CHILD are in the stable.)

COLL   God's dear Dominus. What was that song ?
     It was a wonder curious, wi' small notes among.   320
     I pray to God save us now in this throng.
     I am feared, by Jesus, sommat be wrong.
      I thought
     Someone cried out loud,
     In my ears it rowed -
     I suppose it were a cloud;
      But now there is nought.

GIB   Nay, that might not be, right certain I am
     For he spoke to us three, just like a man.
     When he lightened this lea, me heart raced and ran: 330
     An angel was he - tell thee I can -
      No doubt.
     A bairn newly born
     He said, on this morn -

We must seek him, I warn;
  By yon star that stands out.

DAW   It were a marvel to see; right here to be shown -
It seemed like to me, it had been thunder-flown,
But I saw clear and free as I lay on this stone -
Such a merry glee the best I have known,   340
  I record,
As he said in a scream -
For I'm sure I don't dream -
We should go to Bethleme
To worship that Lord.

(They rise, point their crooks to the East.)

COLL   To so poor as we are that he should appear
We the first to find and be his messenger!

GIB   Come. Let us follow. The place must be near.

DAW   I am ready and eager. Let's go together
  To that light   350

(The SHEPHERDS move to stable and kneel.)

COLL   Hail, comely and clean. Hail young child.
Hail, Maker, as I mean of maiden so mild.
Confounded he's been, that Warlock so wild:
That serpent unseen, now goes he beguiled.
  Lo! He merries.
Look! He laughs, my sweeting.
How grand is his greeting.
A very fair meeting.
  Have a bob of cherries.

GIB   Hail, sovereign Saviour, for thou hast us sought.   360
Hail, nurseling and flower, that all things has wrought.
Hail, full of favour, that makes all out of nought.
Hail, I kneel and I cower. A bird have I brought
  To my bairn.

Hail! Little tiny mop;
Of our creed thou art crop:
I would drink of thy cup,
Little day starne.

DAW   Hail, little darling dear, full of Godhead.   370
I pray thee be near when that I have need.
Hail, sweet in thy cheer. My heart will bleed
To see thee lie here in so poor weed,
    Wi' no pennies.
Though thy hands are right small,
I bring nobbut a ball
For thee t' play withall;
    And so go to t' tennis.

MARY   The Father of heaven, God omnipotent,
That set all days in seven, His son has He sent.
My name he could name, and on me his light spent.   380
I conceived him full even by God's might as he meant;
    And now he is born.
May He keep you from woe.
I shall pray Him so.
Tell forth as you go,
And think on this morn.

(The SHEPHERDS stand and replace caps.)

COLL   Farewell, Lady, so fair to behold
With thy child on thy knee.

GIB   But he lies full cold.
Lord, all's well wi' me. Now we go, thou behold.

DAW   By gow, already it seems to be told   390
    Full oft;

COLL   What grace we have found.

GIB   Come on! Let's be gone.

DAW   To sing it loud we are bound;
               Let's sing it aloft.

(The musicians play an appropriate song and the SHEPHERDS go off singing as the rest of the cast take away the props and settings, some joining in the song.)

During the shepherds' song, the cast come into the arena with banner, skip, props and setting. The cast put on costumes whilst others position props and so on. As the music ends, PILATE, ANNAS, CAIAPHAS and the FOUR SOLDIERS take their positions.

THE RESURRECTION

PILATE's council chamber.

PILATE   Peace I warn you, judges bold!
          And cease ye moans 'til I have told
          What my state shall unfold
             To all in this place.
          If any dare refuse, behold,
             His bones shall hang high in space.

          Know ye all that I am Pilate,
          That sat in judgement of late
          At Calvary, where I was at
             This day at morn.   10
          I am he, that great state,
             That had the lad all torn.

          Now, sin' that loathed losell's dead,
          I have great joy in my manhead;
          Then would I warn in equal stead
             That all take heed -
          Lest any man thinks to obey that hothead
             Or dare to follow his lead.

          As I am man of mighty most
          If there be any person that such boast,   20
          In dreadful torment shall he be roast
             For evermore.
          The devil to hell shall harry his ghost.
             Need I say more.

CAIAPHAS   Sir, ye have nought to fear,
          The Centurion, I hear,
          Your guard, is still there
             To see that none offend.
          We left him behind as a man most wise,
          If any rebels decide to rise,
          To arrest them for the next assize.   30
             And then make end.

(The CENTURION enters.)

CENTURION   God save you, sirs, on every side!
              Worship and wealth in world so wide!

PILATE   Centurion ! All hail to our sight
              Our comely knight!

CENTURION   God grant you grace well for to guide
              And rule in full right.

PILATE   Centurion, welcome ! draw near at hand!
              Tell us your tidings to all here among   40
              For you have gone throughout our land
              Ye know every part.

CENTURION   Sir, I fear me you and your throng
              Have done wondrous wrong.

CAIAPHAS   Wondrous wrong ? I pray thee why ?
              Declare it to this company.

CENTURION   So shall I, sir, tell you truly
              With all my main;
              A righteous man is he say I
              That ye have slain.   50

PILATE   Centurion. No more such jaw;
              Ye are a noble man of our law,
              And should we any witness draw,
                 Us to excuse,
              To maintain us evermore ye owe
                 And not refuse.

CENTURION   To maintain truth is very worthy;
              I said when I saw him die
              That He was God's son almighty
                 That hanged there;   60
              So say I still, and will stand by
                 That fore'er.

ANNAS   Thou, sir! Such statements ye may rue,
Thou shouldst not repeat such news
Unless thou could any tokens true
    Unto us tell.

CENTURION   Such wonderful events never yet ye knew
As then befell.

The sun for woe did lose its light,
The moon and stars ne'er shone at night;   70
The earth trembled as it might
    Begin to speak.
Great stones, that never stirred before then,
    Asunder smashed and break;
And dead men rose up bodily, both great and small

PILATE   Centurion! Beware withall!
Ye know our clerics eclipses call
    Such sudden sight;
Both sun and moon that season shall
    Lack of their light.   80

CAIAPHAS   Aye ! And if that dead men rose up bodily
That may've been done through sorcery;
Therefore set we nothing thereby
    That casts thee down.

CENTURION   Sir, that I saw truly
That shall I evermore own.

PILATE   Harlot! Wherefore doth thou come here
With such lies to feed our ear ?
Go hence ! Or hang high tha' might I swear
    Vile slut.   90

CAIAPHAS   Be off! And i' this troublesome time o' t' year
    Keep your mouth shut.

CENTURION   Sirs, sin' ye believe me not, have a good day!
God give you grace enough to know the truth anyway.

(Exit CENTURION.)

CAIAPHAS	But sithee beware of more doubt
	That, spreading, might force us out:
	Therefore, sir, while you're about
	Among us all,
	Tell us of these tales they shout -
	How they will fall.

100

For Jesus said full openly,
Unto the men that follow him by -
A thing that grieves all Jewry
    If it so may -
That he should rise up bodily
    Within the third day.

If it be so, and that's what I read,
There's more to dread i' t' latter deed
Than in t' first, if we take heed
    And notice thereto;

110

Tell us, Sir, for we have need,
    The best thing to do.

ANNAS	Sir, nevertheless if he said so,
	He hasn't the might to rise up and go;
	But if his disciples steal his corse though,
	And bear it away,
	That were to us a terrible blow -
	A foul affray.

For then would they say, everyone,
That he were risen hisself alone,

120

Therefore, gi' command to keep that stone
    Guarded with knights
'Til three days be come and gone
    And all's brought to rights.

PILATE	Now certainly, sirs, right well ye say,
	And for this same point to purvey
	I shall, and that I may;

He shall not rise,
Nor none shall steal him thence away
  In no kind wise. 130

Sir knights, that are of deeds doughty
Chosen chiefly for your chivalry,
As I may me on you rely,
  Both day and night
Go ye and guard Jesu's body
  With all your might.

And whatever else you may
Guard him well 'til the third day,
That no traitor take his corpse away
  Out of that tomb. 140
For, if they do, truly I say,
  Ye shall be doomed.

FIRST KNIGHT Yea, sir Pilate, thou'rt right !
  We shall him guard with all our might;
There shall no traitor day or night
  Him from us steal.
And we shall break him with great fright
  Whoso comes here.

The scene moves to the tomb which they approach.

SECOND KNIGHT Who should sit where, I'd like to know.

FIRST KNIGHT E'en on this side will I go. 150

THIRD KNIGHT And shall I by his feet - or maybe no !

FOURTH KNIGHT We curse thee there!
  Now, by the rood, I'd like to know
  Who dares steal here.

(They sleep : ANGELS descend and sing : JESUS appears to them.)

JESUS Earthly man that I have wrought,

Wightly awake, and sleep thou nought!
With bitter grief I have thee bought
   To make thee free;
Into this dungeon deep I sought
   And all for love of thee.   160

A crown of thorns, with points so keen,
They set upon my head for teen;
Two thieves hang they me between,
   All for spite;
This pain I have thought I to save
   Mans soul from Hell.

Behold my body, Jews beat it strong
With knotted whips and scourged thong;
As streams of well, the blood out sprung
   On every side;   170
Knots where they hit, well may thou know,
   Made wounds more wide.

Nought else but love ask I of thee
And that thou try hard sin to flee;
Strive thee to live in charity
   Both night and day;
Then in my bliss that never shall miss
   Thou shall dwell aye.

For I am the very prince of peace,
And from many sins I may release,   180
And whoso will of sinning cease
   And mercy cry,
I grant them here a dish
   In bread, mine own body.

That same very bread of life
Becomes my flesh in words fife;
Who so it receives in sin or strife
   Is dead for ever;
But who so it takes in righteous life
   Die shall he never.   190

(JESUS vanishes. The THREE MARYS enter the garden.)

MAGDALENE   Alas, to die with grief am I dight
          In world was never more woeful wight;
          I droop, I tremble, at the awful sight
             That I have seen;
          My Lord, that great was of might,
             Is dead for me.

MARY   Alas, how stand I on my feet
          When I think on his wounds wet!
          Jesus that was of love so sweet
             And never did ill,
          Is dead and graven beneath the stone
             Withouten skill.   200

SALOME   Withouten reason these Jews, each one,
          That lovely lord they have him slain,
          And trespass did he never none,
             In no kind of stead;
          To whom shall we now make our moan ?
             Our Lord is dead.

MAGDALENE   Since he is dead, my sisters dear,
          Let's leave here with full good cheer   210
          With our anointments fair and clear
             That we have brought,
          For to anoint his wounds severe
             That Jews him wrought.

MARY   Go we then, my sisters free,
          For sure me craves his corse to see.

MAGDALENE   Sisters, we might no further go
          Ne'er make mourning;
          I see two sitting where we're going to,
             In white clothing.   220

MARY   Certain, the truth we cannot hide,
          The grave stone is put aside.

SALOME Sure, for thing that may betide,
     Now will we wend
    To seek our love, and with him bide
     That was our friend.

(They approach the ANGELS.)

ANGEL 1 Ye women mourning in your thought,
    Here in this place whom have ye sought ?

MAGDALENE Jesus, that to death was brought,
     Our Lord so free.   230

ANGEL 2 Certain, women, here is he not;
    Come near and see.

ANGEL 1 He is not here, the sooth to say,
    The place is void that in he lay;
    The cloth here see ye may
     Was on him laid;
    He is risen and gone his way,
     As he you said.

ANGEL 2 Even as he said, so done has he,
    He is risen through his power;   240
    He shall be found in Galilee
     In flesh and fell;
    To his disciples now wend ye
     And thus them tell.

MAGDALENE My sisters three, since it is so,
    That he is risen from death thus
    As said to us these angels two,
     Our Lord and leach
    As ye have heard, where e'er ye go
     Look that ye preach.   250

MARY As we have heard, so shall we say;
    Mary, our sister, have a good day!

MAGDALENE   Now truly God, as he well may -
     Man of most might -
     He wish you, sisters, well on your way,
     And rule you right.

(THE THREE MARYS leave. THE SOLDIERS awake and see the tomb is empty.

FIRST KNIGHT Out alas! What shall I say ?
     Where is the corse that herein lay ?

SECOND KNIGHT What ails thee, man ? Is he away
     That we should guard ?   260

FIRST KNIGHT Rise up and see.

SECOND KNIGHT Harrow! For ay
     That'll go hard.

THIRD KNIGHT What the devil ails you two
     Such noise and cry thus for to make ?

SECOND KNIGHT For he is gone.

THIRD KNIGHT Alas! Who ?

SECOND KNIGHT He that here lay.

THIRD KNIGHT Harrow ! Devil !
     How so got he away ?

FIRST KNIGHT Alas, what shall we do this day
     Since this conjurer is gone away
     And safely, sirs, I dare well say   270
     He rose alone.

FOURTH KNIGHT Knew Sir Pilate of this affray
     We mun be slain.

THIRD KNIGHT Aye ! If Sir Pilate learns of this deed

That we were sleeping when he went
We mun forfeit, without dread,
    All life and limb.

FOURTH KNIGHT   We must make up lies, for some we need
        To tell him.   280

THIRD KNIGHT   That read I well, so might I go.

SECOND KNIGHT   And I agree thereto also.

THIRD KNIGHT   A thousand, shall I say, and more,
        Well armed each one,
        Came and took his corpse us fro'
        And had us near slain.

FIRST KNIGHT Nay, certain, I hold there none so good
        As tell the truth even as it stood,
        How that he rose with main and mood,
            And went his way;   290
        To sir Pilate, if he be wooed,
            Thus dare I say.

FOURTH KNIGHT   Why and dare thou to sir Pilate go
        With this tidings and tell him so ?

SECOND KNIGHT   So believe I that we do also;
        We die but once.
        Now he that wrought us all this woe
            Woe to his bones !

FOURTH KNIGHT   Go we then, sir knights all four;
        Sin we shall mek Pilate sour !   300
        Cumbered cowards, he'll call us all.
            Cumbered cowards !

FIRST KNIGHT But still I'll tell each word an' all
        As it happ'ed toward.

PILATE'S council chamber.

(THE FOUR KNIGHTS enter.)

PILATE   You are welcome our knights so keen;
                In mickle mirth may you now be seen.
                But first tell your tale us between
                    How ye have wrought.

FIRST KNIGHT Our task, my lord, withouten doubt
                    Is worthed to nought   31●

CAIAPHAS   To nought ? Alas, what mean these words !

FIRST KNIGHT The prophet, Jesus, that ye well know,
                    Is risen and gone, for all our awe
                      With main and might.

ANNAS   Therefore the devil himself thee draw
                    False recreant knight !

PILATE   Cumbered cowards I ye call !
                Cumbered cowards are ye all !

THIRD KNIGHT   Sir, there was none dare do but small
                    When that he fled.   320

SECOND KNIGHT   We were so feared, down did we fall
                    And quaked for dread.

FOURTH KNIGHT   We were so afraid, everyone,
                    When that he put aside the stone

PILATE   What ! But rose he by himself alone ?

FIRST KNIGHT   Yea, Lord, I fear that's so.

PILATE   Alas, then, are our laws forlorn
                For ever more !
              Ay, devil ! What shall happen now ?

	This world with cunning fares, I trow;	330
	I pray you, Caiaphas, tell me how
	To devise this day.

CAIAPHAS Sir, if I could ought by my wisdom
          Fain would I say.

ANNAS   To say the best forsooth I shall;
          It shall be profit for us all.
          Yon knights behoves their words recall
              How he was missed;
          We would not, for thing that might befall,
              That no man wist.
          And therefore, by your courtesy
          Give them a reward generously.

PILATE   Of this counsel, well paid am I;
              It shall be thus.
          Sir knights, that are in deeds doughty
              Take heed of us;

          Harken now what ye shall say;
          Where so ye go by night or day
          Ten thousand men of good array
              Came you until   350
          With force of arms bore him away
              Against your will.

          Look you say this in every land
          And thereto comes with this command
          A thousand pounds each in your hand
              For your reward;
          And my friendship, you understand,
              Shall not be spared;

FIRST KNIGHT Where so we go where so we wend, this shall we say.

PILATE   The blessing of Mahowne be with you night and day !   360

          (The FOUR KNIGHTS exit.)

PILATE   Thus shall the sooth be bought and sold
                      And treason shall for truth be told.

                      *(PILATE and the others exit as the musicians play a suitable song - perhaps 'Wh**
                      wonrdous love is this?')

The Tomb in the garden.

                      (JESUS, disguised as a gardener, sits by the tomb.)

MARY   *(entering.)*Tell me, gardener, I thee pray,
                      If thou bore ought my Lord away;
                      Tell me the truth, say me no nay,
                         Where that he lies,
                      And I shall remove him if I may,
                         In any kind wise.

JESUS   Woman, why weepest thou ? Be still !
                      Whom seekest thou ? Tell me thy will,   37(
                      Deny me not with nay.

MAGDALENE   For my Lord I look full ill;
                      The place thou bore his body till
                       Tell me I pray;

                      And I shall, if I may, his body bare with me
                      Unto my ending day the better shall I be.

JESUS   Woman; woman. Turn thy thought!
                      Know thou well I hid him not
                      Then bore him away with me;
                      Go seek; look if thou find him ought.   380

MAGDALENE   In faith I have him sought
                      But nowhere he will found be.

JESUS   Why, what was he to thee
                      in soothfastness to say ?

MAGDALENE   Ah, he was to me -

(She falters and makes to leave.)

No longer stay I may.

JESUS   Mary, thou seeks thy God, and that am I.

(JESUS drops his disguise.)

MAGDALENE   Robany, my Lord so dear !
Now am I whole that thou art here
Suffer me to nigh thee near,   390
And kiss thy feet;
Might I do so, so well me were,
For thou art sweet.

JESUS   May, Mary, nigh thou not me,
For to my Father, tell I thee,
Yet ascend I nought;
Tell my brothers I shall be
Before them all in Trinity,
Whose will that I have wrought.

Mary, thou shall wend me fro';   400
To my disciples say thou so,
That baffled are and wrapped in woe,
That I they succour shall.
By name Peter thou call
And say that I shall be
Before him and them all
Myself in Galilee.

(JESUS vanishes.)

MAGDALENE   To Galilee now will I fare,
And his disciples call from care;
I know that they will mourn no more: 410
Returned is their bliss.
That worthy child that Mary bore
He amend your mis.

(The musicians repeat the previous tune as MAGDALENE goes off. The ca
change costume and remove props and setting, some singing the song.)

END

THE JUDGEMENT

There is a fanfare. The cast disperse to their positions as GOD is revealed in a similar position to the beginning of The Creation.

GOD   First when I this world had wrought
Wood and wind and waters wan
And everything that now is ought
Full well, me thought that I did then.
When they were made, good me them thought;
Then to my likeness made I man.
And man to grieve me cared he nought;
Therefore me rues that I the world began.

When I had made man in my guise,
I gave him wits himself to wiss   10
And put him I in Paradise
And bade him hold it all as his.
But of the tree of good and ill
I said 'What time thou eat of this,
Man, thou speeds thy self to spill,
Thou art brought out of all bliss.'

Straightway broke man my bidding;
He would have been a god thereby !
He would have knowledge of every thing,
In world to be as wise as I.   20
He ate the apple I had bade should lie,
Thus was he beguiled through gluttony.
Then both him and all his fry,
To pine for ay I put on he.

Too long and late me thought it good
To catch those caitiffs out of care;
I sent my son with full blithe mood
To earth, to save them of their sare
For ruth of them he rests on rood
And bought them with his body bare.   30
For them he shed his heart and blood;
What kindness might I do them more ?

Since then have they found me full of mercy,
Full of grace and forgiveness,

And they as wretches, wittingly,
Have led their life in idleness.
Oft have they grieved me grievously,
Thus have they quit me my kindness;
Therefore no longer, certainly,
Suffer will I their wickedness.

I have suffered mankind many a year
In lust and liking for to lend,
And hardly find I, far or near,
A man that will his wickedness amend
On earth I see sin everywhere,
Therefore my angels will I send
To blow their horns that all may hear
The time is come I will make end.

Angels, blow your trumpets straight
Every creature for to call;
Learned and crude, both man and mate,
Reserve their doom this day they shall;
Every lad that ever had life,
Be none forgotten, great nor small.
There shall they see the wounds five
That my son suffered for them all.

And separate them before my sight;
Together in bliss shall they not be.
My blessed childer as I have hight
On my right hand I shall them see:
Then shall each a cursed wight
On my left side in terror flee.
This day their dooms thus have I dight
To each a man as he hath served me.

(GOD exits.)

MICHAEL   Loved be thou, Lord of most mightiest
That angel made to messenger !
Thy will shall be fulfilled in haste,
That Heaven and Earth and Hell shall hear.

Good and ill, every each ghost
Rise and fetch your flesh, that death did tear   70
For all this world is brought to waste;
Draw to your doom, the end is near.

GABRIEL   Every creature, both old and offspring,
Straightway, I bid you that ye rise,
Body and soul with you ye bring
And come before the high justice.
For I am sent from heaven's king
To call you to this great assize.
Therefore rise up and give reckoning
How ye him served upon many wise.   80

*(There is a prolonged and awful blast on the trumpets/horns and the dead souls
arise in a manner reminiscent of ADAM and EVE'S creation.)*

BAD SOULS   Ah, ah, ah ! cleave asunder bodies of clay
Asunder break to let souls pass
Alas ! Alas ! and wellaway !
That we were born, alack alas !

BAD SOUL 1   So may we sinful wretches say
I hear well by this hideous horn
It draws full near to doomsday.
Alas, we wretches that are forlorn

BAD SOUL 2   What shall we wretches do for dread
Or whether for fear we may flee   90
When we may bring forth no good deed
Before him that our judge shall be ?

BAD SOUL 3   To ask mercy us is no need
For well I wot we damned be.
Alas ! That we such life should lead
That dight us has this destiny.

Of wicked works they will us accuse,
That we thought never had we been known,
Those that we did aft full privately,

Openly may we see them known.

BAD SOUL 2 Alas ! For dread sore may we quake,
Our deeds be our own damnation,
In Hell to dwell with fiends black,
Where never shall be redemption.

BAD SOUL 4 Alas, careworn caitiffs may we rise;
Sore may we wring our hands and weep;
For being cursed and covetous,
Damned be we in Hell full deep.

BAD SOUL 3 Cared we never for God's service;
His commandments would we nothing keep,
But oft that made we sacrifice
To Satan, when others sleep.

BAD SOUL 1 Alas, now wakens all our fear !
Our wicked deeds may we not hide,
But on our backs us must them bear;
They will us destroy on either side.

BAD SOULS Before us clearly shall be forth brought
The deeds that shall ourselves damned be -
That ears have heard, or heart has thought,
That mouths have spoke or eye has seen,
This day full dear then is it bought.

ANGEL Stand nought together, part you in two;

(Separates GOOD from BAD SOULS.)

Together shall ye nought be in bliss;
My father of Heaven will it be so,
For many of you has wrought amiss.
The good, on his right hand ye go,
The way to Heaven he will you show;
Ye wicked men, ye flee him fro'
On his left hand, as none of his.

JESUS   This woeful world is brought to end,
My Father of Heaven he wills it be;   130
Therefore to earth now will I wend,
Myself to sit in majesty.
To deem my dooms I will descend;
This body will I bear with me,
How it was decreed, mans ills to mend,
All mankind there shall it see.

(JESUS comes down to earth.)

My apostles who by me bided near
The dreadful doom this day is dight.
Both Heaven and Earth and Hell shall hear
How I shall hold that I have hight   140
That ye shall sit beside me here,
Beside myself to see that sight,
And for to doom folk far and near,
After their working, wrong or right.

PETER   Late and early, loud and still,
To do thy bidding am I ready;
I oblige me to do thy will,
With all my might, as is worthy.

(PETER sits on JESUS's right side and MARY on his left.)

GABRIEL   Believe, believe, and make your way
One and all before the throne.   150
Come at last is judgement day
To make some glad, and other some groan.

MICHAEL   Believe, believe, and make your way;
Why do ye all not leand your ear ?
Come is the day of wealth and woe;
Go thither now your doom to hear.

BOTH ANGELS Believe, believe, why do ye stay
When Doomsday's horn doth ye now call?

Come at last is judgement day
Go, as we bade ye, one and all.

(The jaws of Hell open and the DEVILS enter. Each carries an unlit power torch disguised as a tormentor.)

1st DEVIL   Fellows, prepare us for to fight;
                   And go we fast our riches to take;
                   The dreadful doom this day is dight;
                   I dread me that we dwell too long.

2nd DEVIL   We shall be seen ever in their sight,
                   And warily wait, or else we wrang
                   For if the doomsman do us right
                   Full great part with us shall gang.

3rd DEVIL   He shall do right to foe and friend,
                   For now shall all the truth be sought
                   All worried men with us shall wend
                   To pain endless their shall be brought.

(The musicians play and the end of the world is seen; Mappa Mundi is broke two as JESUS speaks over.)

JESUS   *(In judgement.)*
                   Every creature take entent,
                   What warnings I to you bring.
                   This woeful world away is went
                   And I am come as crowned king.
                   My Father in Heaven, he has me sent
                   To judge your deeds and make ending.
                   Come is the day of judgement;
                   Of sorrow must each a sinner sing.

                   The day is come of wretchedness,
                   Bring care to them that are unclean,
                   The day of bale and bitterness,
                   Full long awaited has it been,
                   The day of dread to more and less,
                   Of care, of trembling and of wrath.

That each a creature that wearied is
May say, 'Alas, the day I lived to seen !'

Here may ye see my wounds wide,
The which I suffered for your misdeed,   190
Through heart and head, foot hand and hide,
Not for my guilt, but for your need.
Behold both body, back and side,
How dear I bought your brotherhood.
These bitter pains I would abide
To buy you bliss, thus would I bleed.

My body was scourged withouten skill;
As thief full slave-like was I treaten;
On cross they hanged me, on a hill,
Bloody and blue, as I was beaten.   200
With crown of thorns thrust full ill;
This spear unto my side was pierced;
Mine heart blood spared nought they for to spill;
Man, for thy love would I no let.

Thus was I dight thy sorrow to slake;
Man, thus behold thee to saved be .
In all my woe took I no wrake
My will it was for the love of thee.
Man, sore aught thee for to quake,
This dreadful day this sight to see.   210
All this I suffered for thy sake;
Say, man, what suffered thou for me ?

(To GOOD SOULS.)

My blessed children on my right hand,
Your doom this day ye need not fear,
For all your comforts is coming;
Your life in liking shall ye lead.
Come to the Kingdom ay lasting,
That you in dight for your good deed;
Full glad may ye be where ye stand
For great in Heaven shall be your reward.   220

When I was hungry, ye me fed;
To slake my thirst your heart was free;
When I was clothless ye me clad;
Ye would no sorrow upon me see.
In hard prison when I was pressed
Of my pains ye had pity;
Full sick when I was brought to bed
Kindly ye came to comfort me.

When I was weak and weariest
Ye sheltered me full heartfully;
Full glad then were ye of your guest,
And pitied my poverty piteously.
Swiftly ye brought me of the best,
And made my bed full easily;
Therefore in Heaven shall be your rest,
In joy and bliss to be me by.

GOOD SOUL 1   When had we, Lord that all has wrought,
Meat and drink thee with to feed,
Sin we on earth had never nought
But through the grace of thy Godhead ?

GOOD SOUL 2   When was it that we the clothes brought,
Or visit thee in any need,
Or in thy sickness we thee sought
Lord, when did we thee this deed ?

JESUS   My blessed bairns, I shall you say
What time this deed was to me done:
When any that need had, night or day,
Asked your help and had it soon.
Your free heart said them never nay,
Early or late, midday nor noon
But as oft times as they would pray,
They only to ask, and have it done.

(He turns to the BAD SOULS.)

Ye cursed caitiffs of Cain's kind
That never me comforts in my care,
I and ye for ever will twain
In dole to dwell for evermore;
Your bitter bales shall never blin,
That ye shall have when ye come there.
Thus have ye served for your sin.
For wicked deeds ye have done ere.   260

When I had need of meat and drink,
Caitiffs, ye cast me from your gate;
When ye were sat as sirs on bench,
I stood thereout, weary and wet,
Was none of you would on me think,
Pity to have of my poor state;
Therefore to Hell I shall you sink,
Well are ye worthy to go to that gate.

When I was sick and sorriest,
Ye visited me nought, for I was poor;   270
In prison fast when I was fest
Was none of you looked how I fared.
When I knew never where for to rest,
With blows you drove me from your door;
But ever to pride then were ye pressed;
My flesh, my blood often ye foreswore.

Clothless when I was often and cold,
In need of you went I full naked;
House nor shelter, help nor hold
Had I none of you, though I quaked   280
My trouble saw ye many fold
Was none of you my sorrow slaked,
But ever forsook me, young and old;
Therefore shall ye now be forsaken.

BAD SOUL 1   When had thou, Lord that all thing has,
Hunger or thirst, sin thou God art ?
When was it thou in prison was,
When was thou naked or shelterless ?

BAD SOUL 2 When was it we saw thee sick, alas ?
      What showed we thee this unkindness,
      Weary or wet too let thee pass
      When did we this wickedness ?

JESUS   Caitiffs, as oft as it betid
      That the needful aught asked in my name,
      Ye heard them nought, your ears ye hid,
      Your help to them was not at home,
      To me was that unkindness bid.
      Therefore ye bear this bitter blame,
      To least or most when ye it did,
      To me ye did the self and the same.

      (He turns to the GOOD SOULS.)

      My chosen children, come unto me;
      With me to dwell now shall ye wend;
      There joy and bliss shall ever be;

      (GOOD SOULS go to Heaven.)

      Your life in liking shall ye lend.

      (He turns once more to the BAD SOULS.)

      Ye cursed caitiffs, from me ye flee,
      In Hell to dwell withouten end.
      There ye shall never but sorrow see,
      And sit by Satan the fiend.

      (As JESUS, PETER, MARY and THE GOOD SOULS ascend to heaven, th
      DEVILS and BAD SOULS gather together and stare at the audience, the
      address them in an accusing manner. They shine their torches into th
      audience.)

DEVILS   We feel foul fiends that will us fear,
      And all for pomp and wicked pride;
      Weep we may with many a tear.
      Alas, that we this day should bide.

(Suddenly, the DEVILS go among the audience pointing torches from person to person.)

FIRST DEVIL *(to a member of audience)*
I have here writ on thy forehead
Thou wert vain and full of pride.
(to another)
Thou wouldst not give a poor man bread
But from thy door thou did him chide.

SECOND DEVIL *(to another member of audience)*
And in thy face I do here read
That if a thirsty man come to any tide
Even though he should be well nigh dead
Drink from him thoud'st ever hide.   320

THIRD DEVIL *(to yet another member of audience.)*
Evermore on envy was all thy mind
Thou wouldst never visit no prisoner
(to another) To all thy neighbours thou were unkind.
Thou wouldst never help a man in danger.

FIRST DEVIL   The sin of sloth, thy soul shall shend
Nor mass nor matins would thou hear
And mercy is we shall it lack
Our sins are written down in black.

SECOND DEVIL Thou hadst rejoice in gluttony
In drunkenness and ribaldry.   330

THIRD DEVIL   Now the fires of hell draw nigh
And thou shalt know no rest.

FIRST DEVIL   God's men you loved but few.

SECOND DEVIL Those in need you never nursed

THIRD DEVIL   Not even now a drop of dew
Shall quench thy everlasting thirst.

DEVILS *(who have returned to acting area.)*

> But, sirs, we you all tell,
> If doomsday had come much later,
> Then we'd have to build our hell

FIRST DEVIL   Grimmer...

SECOND DEVIL   grander...

ALL *(shout)*   greater!

(LUCIFER has entered among the Bad Souls. He now bursts through them a addresses the audience. The devils spotlight him with torches.)

LUCIFER   Ye adulterers, lechers all
> Your bale now brews
> Your pleasures fall.
> Every harlot who lures
> Each bawd that procuress
> Welcome to my hall.
>
> Ye liars and lubbers, all who thieve,
> All ill-tempered knifers many grieve,
> Extortioners and wreckers I gladly receive,
> Usurers and jurors who by bribery cleave,
> With me ye are to dwell'
>
> Also gamesters and dicers
> Slanderers and backbiters
> Welcome to my Hell !

(There is a burst of music as the BAD SOULS are ushered protesting loudly in Hell by the DEVILS and LUCIFER. thewir is screaming and cries for help. Th doors of hell slam to and the screams are silenced. GOD appears in front heaven in a warm shaft of light.)

GOD   Now is fulfilled all my forethought,
> For ended is all earthly thing,
> All worldly beings that I have wrought,

	After their works have now winning;	
	They that would sin and ceased nought,	
	Of sorrows many shall they now sing,	360

JESUS   And they that mended them whilst they ought,
         Shall build and bide in my blessing.

(The spot light on GOD fades.)

(A LONE SINGER, high up, is lit by a single pink spot as GOD and JESUS retreat into heaven.)

SINGER *(unaccompanied)* This aye neet
         This aye neet
         Every neet an' all.
         Fire and fleet and candle leet.
         And Christ tek up thy soul

(The musicians take up the tune and the whole cast enter from Heaven and Hell, and from 'the wings' into the acting arena, some with banners drooped. They all sing the song.

There is a short pause.
The musicians break into the dance tune or jig played at the opening of the play and the cast gather up their things, chat to the audience and wish them a pleasant journey, and so on, as they go off with skips and props in an informal procession waving goodbye as they go.)

END